Library Technology REPORTS
Expert Guides to Library Systems and Services

3-D Printers for Libraries

Jason Griffey

ALA TechSource
alatechsource.org

American Library Association

Library Technology Reports

ALA TechSource purchases fund advocacy, awareness, and accreditation programs for library professionals worldwide.

Volume 50, Number 5
3-D Printers for Libraries
ISBNs: (print) 978-0-8389-5930-5; (PDF) 978-0-8389-5931-2; (ePub) 978-0-8389-5932-9; (Kindle) 978-0-8389-5933-6.

American Library Association
50 East Huron St.
Chicago, IL 60611-2795 USA
alatechsource.org
800-545-2433, ext. 4299
312-944-6780
312-280-5275 (fax)

Advertising Representative
Patrick Hogan
phogan@ala.org
312-280-3240

Editor
Patrick Hogan
phogan@ala.org
312-280-3240

Copy Editor
Judith Lauber

Production and Design
Tim Clifford, Production Editor
Karen Sheets de Gracia, Manager of Design and Composition

Library Technology Reports (ISSN 0024-2586) is published eight times a year (January, March, April, June, July, September, October, and December) by American Library Association, 50 E. Huron St., Chicago, IL 60611. It is managed by ALA TechSource, a unit of the publishing department of ALA. Periodical postage paid at Chicago, Illinois, and at additional mailing offices. POSTMASTER: Send address changes to Library Technology Reports, 50 E. Huron St., Chicago, IL 60611.

Trademarked names appear in the text of this journal. Rather than identify or insert a trademark symbol at the appearance of each name, the authors and the American Library Association state that the names are used for editorial purposes exclusively, to the ultimate benefit of the owners of the trademarks. There is absolutely no intention of infringement on the rights of the trademark owners.

ALA TechSource
alatechsource.org

Copyright © 2014 Jason Griffey
Licensed under Creative Commons Attribution-NonCommercial 4.0 International (CC BY-NC 4.0).
http://creativecommons.org/licenses/by-nc/4.0/

About the Author

Jason Griffey is the founder and principal consultant at Evenly Distributed (http://evenlydistributed.net), a technology consulting firm for libraries and education. He has written extensively on libraries and technology, most recently a chapter in *The Top Technologies Every Librarian Needs to Know: A LITA Guide*. His previous book, *Mobile Technology and Libraries*, is a part of the award-winning Tech Set series. Named a *Library Journal* Mover & Shaker in 2009, Griffey has written and spoken internationally on topics such as the future of technology and libraries, personal electronics in the library, privacy, copyright, and intellectual property. Griffey is the designer and director of The LibraryBox Project (http://librarybox.us), an open-source portable digital file distribution system.

Abstract

Library Technology Reports (vol. 50, no. 5) "3-D Printers for Libraries" offers an explanation of the various types of 3-D printers, how they work, and the materials used. The Report describes a range of specific 3-D printing products appropriate for library use.

Get Your *Library Technology Reports* Online!

Subscribers to ALA TechSource's *Library Technology Reports* can read digital versions, in PDF and HTML formats, through the scholarly content host MetaPress. Subscribers also have access to an archive of past issues. Visit alatechsource.metapress.com to begin reading. Beside each issue title you will see a solid green box indicating that it is available to you. You may need to log in to be recognized by the system. Please contact MetaPress Support, support@metapress.com, if you have any questions about or problems with access.

Subscriptions
alatechsource.org/subscribe

Contents

Chapter 1—Introduction — 5
- What Is 3-D Printing? — 5
- Library-Specific Issues — 6
- The Case for 3-D Printing in Libraries — 6
- Conclusion — 7
- Notes — 7

Chapter 2—The Types of 3-D Printing — 8
- Fused Deposition Modeling Printing — 8
- Stereolithography — 11
- Selective Laser Sintering — 11
- Laminated Object Manufacturing — 12
- Other 3-D Printing Types — 12

Chapter 3—Types of Plastics — 13
- ABS — 13
- PLA — 14
- Other Plastics — 14
- Notes — 15

Chapter 4—Creating and Printing Files — 16
- File Formats — 16
- Design Software — 17
- 3-D Scanning — 18
- Operational Software — 20

Chapter 5—3-D Printers — 23
- MakerBot — 23
- LulzBot — 25
- Printrbot — 26
- Solidoodle — 26
- SeeMeCNC Rostock Max and Orion — 26
- Hyrel 3D — 27
- Cubify — 28
- Formlabs — 28
- Old World Laboratories — 29
- Mcor — 29

Chapter 1

Introduction

Abstract

Chapter 1 of Library Technology Reports *(vol. 50, no. 5) "3-D Printers for Libraries" explains the mechanical process of a 3-D printer. Author Jason Griffey raises a few library-specific issues and makes an argument for libraries to implement 3-D printing.*

Over the last two to three years, there has been an explosion of interest in 3-D printing in libraries. This has been driven by the falling cost of the technology and the rise in interest in interactive, creative spaces inside libraries (makerspaces or tinkerlabs). 3-D printing as a technology isn't new; it's been available commercially for decades. But only in the last five years or so has the price for deposition printers, driven by dedicated hobbyists and the company MakerBot Industries, dropped to the point where they are within the reach of the average individual.

There are a number of reasons that libraries should be looking at 3-D printing as an addition to their technology services. The first is that libraries, especially public libraries, have often been a technological leveler for their communities. Libraries were the first place where many people came to print their résumés on a laser printer. (It's easy to forget how transformative high-quality printing was in the late 1980s.) They were also the first place where many people had an experience with the Internet, especially with the World Wide Web, in the mid-1990s. Going back to pre-computer technologies, the local public library was the place where someone could go and use a typewriter that was freely available. So libraries have a well-worn history of being places where new technologies can be seen and interacted with for the first time. 3-D printers are at the point now where the personal computer was in 1984; they are mostly a hobbyist pursuit, but they have a clear future.

That future is as varied as the objects these printers can create. There are a number of traditional mechanisms for creating things in plastic, ranging from machining and milling (subtractive manufacturing) to molding and vacuum forming. In most cases, these are optimized for creating a high volume of identical plastic parts, such as tens of thousands of action figures or hundreds of thousands of appliance parts. They are almost impossible to use cost-effectively if you want just one of something, and that's where 3-D printing shines. With a 3-D printer, you can create unlimited numbers of unique objects for the same price. Need a replacement part for a toy? No problem. And then when you need a doorstop or a speaker frame or something totally other, that's not a problem either. If you're making ten thousand copies of a thing, there are more cost-effective options. But if you need just one, there is no better option than printing it.

This flexibility is key to the uptake of the technology, especially in libraries. Each patron can design and create his or her own particular object. Kids can print new additions to the toys that they love and can create just about anything that they can imagine.

What Is 3-D Printing?

The simplest way to imagine a 3-D printer is that it's a machine that makes bigger things out of smaller blocks. In some cases, the "blocks" are a powder; in others, they are melted plastic; and in yet others, they are an ultraviolet light–sensitive resin, but in every case it's just a matter of large things being made from smaller substrates. A 3-D printer is a simple sort of robot that understands how to manipulate the raw material it's working with in three dimensions rather than just two, as an ink-jet or laser printer does. This type of manufacturing is also called *additive manufacturing*, as opposed to more traditional subtractive manufacturing where material is removed from a larger sample to create custom shapes in a process like milling, lathing, or CNC (computing numerical control) machines.

Imagine that you take an ink-jet printer, and instead of printing ink, it extrudes hot plastic that cools quickly. Think of it like a hot glue gun, where the plastic is solid, then gets heated to a liquid state, and then cools again into a solid. If it printed this plastic onto a piece of paper, you'd end up with a slightly raised design being "drawn" on the paper by the printhead moving back and forth across the paper (the X dimension) and the paper being moved through the print area (the Y dimension). Those of us old enough to remember the days when color printing was very expensive might have memories of hot-wax printers that did basically this.

With a 3-D printer, you add the last of the spatial dimensions, height, by moving the printhead and printing surface (usually called the *build platform* in this case) apart from each other. In our ink-jet analogy, imagine that you put the printhead on an elevator that could move it closer and farther away from the paper. If you do that while the printhead is putting down plastic, you can just keep moving them farther and farther apart, layer after layer, in the Z dimension. Over time, you end up with an object made of very thin layers of this plastic. That's what most 3-D printing is like.

This is the basis for almost all of the 3-D printing that you have seen in the media over the last few years and almost all of the 3-D printing that libraries have been involved with. As we'll learn in chapter 2, this isn't the only type of 3-D printing—it's just the most affordable.

Library-Specific Issues

Anyone who has talked with people about 3-D printing has probably heard the question, "So can you print a gun with it?" This is by far the most common question I get asked when I'm showing off a 3-D printer, whether it's to students or adults. It's good to have a standard answer to this question, as it's definitely going to come up. Mine is usually, "Maybe, but it would easier and cheaper to make one in a machine shop." This sort of question can also come from people like your friends group or your board, and for that, you might want to have a slightly more nuanced answer that includes things like, "Not really, and it's really not any more dangerous than having chemistry textbooks on the shelves."

Other objections to having a 3-D printer in the library include the overall cost of the consumable filament, which is easily recouped by charging just a few pennies per ounce for prints. The staff skills necessary are a concern, as 3-D printing really is at the level of hobbyist at this point. I often tell people that running a 3-D printer is like driving a classic car. You can do it even if you don't know anything, but it'll be a whole lot cheaper if you can change the oil yourself. For a 3-D printer, that might include regular cleaning, bed leveling, and occasionally swapping out a part if necessary.

Other skills that are useful but not necessary would include having someone who is at least aware of the types of modeling programs and could troubleshoot basic things like, "That won't print because of X reason." Libraries might also want to provide their patrons with resources for learning more, so it's a good idea to purchase materials about 3-D printing, modeling, and the like in case you have a patron who wants to deep-dive into the topic.

The Case for 3-D Printing in Libraries

The question that comes up most often, after the gun question, when I talk to librarians about 3-D printing is the very practical "Why?" Why 3-D printing in libraries? Why should libraries spend money and time on providing these services to the public?

There are a variety of ways to answer this question, but I think that the most straightforward is, "We've always done this sort of thing." Libraries are, at their core, an engine of democratization of knowledge and information. The library as a concept acts as a collective resource for the individuals of a community, and while we are best known for the resource of information, that's never been all we are. Libraries were often the first place in a community where someone could go to touch a computer and were one of the places where most Americans first saw the Internet. Those of us who were around technology in the 1990s remember how amazing something as omnipresent as a laser printer was in its early days. The library was often the place where patrons would go to print their résumés in the early 1990s because they didn't have a printer at home and the laser printer looked so much more professional than the more common dot-matrix printers. Even further back than the computer, the library was the place where members of the community could use a typewriter.

The point is that the library has a long, long history of providing technology for its patrons. It is still admittedly early in the life of 3-D printing, but the basic technology is affordable at this point. The future of additive manufacturing is likely to be stranger and more wonderful than I can imagine, but given the ways that even these very rough first steps are being used (in health care to print organs, in food prep to make unique foodstuffs, in art to make impossible objects), I think it's fair to say that some amazing things will come from this technology.

To give you some idea of the sorts of things that are possible with 3-D printing technology, there are hundreds of inspiring stories around the web—some that are barely believable. Here are just a few:

- 3-D printed tissues and structures have already been implanted successfully into humans, and the potential for printing entire replacement organs is on the horizon.[1]
- People are using 3-D printers to provide custom, cheaper, and more comfortable prostheses for amputees and children, providing them with hugely better living conditions.[2]
- The same technique used in FDM printing (fused deposition modeling, discussed in chapter 2) is being used to build experimental housing and could revolutionize low-cost housing, including replacement housing after natural disasters.[3]

I also believe strongly that it would benefit libraries themselves to have 3-D printers available for any number of reasons. While it's great to provide the technology to patrons, don't forget that libraries and librarians could benefit from it as well. Need a shelf bracket? Want to have a custom sign for your new books shelf? How about a custom sign for every month? Need to repair a random broken plastic thing? Once you have the power to create arbitrary things, the benefit is that you can create anything you can think of.

Give access to a 3-D printer to your public services department, to your circulation department; see what they can imagine that would make their jobs easier. Then share that thing for other libraries to print. If libraries started iterating things that improve librarians' daily tasks, everyone could benefit. And 3-D printers help enable that kind of thinking—the ability to see a thing in the world and want to make it better. That's what I want to see libraries and librarians working toward.

Conclusion

The ultimate promise of this technology is the Replicator from *Star Trek*, a machine capable of taking the raw building blocks of matter at the atomic level and recombining them into anything you can imagine. That is obviously not happening soon, but this is how we get there, by building the simple machines that help illuminate the way.

Libraries have always been a place for their communities to discover new things. As technologies become increasingly important for accessing information and interacting with the world, libraries have become a place where people can go to see The New. 3-D printing is one of many technologies that are going to help to define the future in many ways, from fundamentally changing aspects of medicine to reworking the way we think about manufacturing.

Note that I am not saying that every library needs to immediately run out and purchase a 3-D printer. Many already have, and more have plans to, either through staff interest or through actual patron demand. I think that 3-D printers, in one form or another, will eventually become as commonplace as laser printers. Not everyone will have one at home, but most people will have access to one if they need it. And a lot of that access may come through their public library.

As the technology becomes more fully featured, as the 3-D printers become capable of printing more and more complicated objects, and as the prices continue to drop, more and more people will see that these devices may fill a need in their lives: not necessarily owning a printer, but being aware of their capabilities and able to imagine using one. That is also an opportunity for some public libraries, to be ready for that potential by understanding the current state of the 3-D printing landscape. It's always easier to be ready for the future when you prepare for it in the present.

Notes

1. Anthony Atala, "Lungs on a Chip, 3-D Printed Hearts: The Shape of Medicine to Come," Vital Signs, CNN Opinion, March 13, 2014, www.cnn.com/2014/03/12/opinion/lungs-chip-3-D-print-organs; Susan Young Rojahn, "Artificial Organs May Finally Get a Blood Supply," *MIT Technology Review*, March 6, 2014, www.technologyreview.com/news/525161/artificial-organs-may-finally-get-a-blood-supply.
2. Marcus Wohlsen, "The Next Big Thing You Missed: 3-D Printing Promises Better Bionic Limbs for the War-Wounded," *Wired*, March 18, 2014, www.wired.com/2014/03/next-big-thing-missed-bionic-limbs-3D-printed-worlds-war-wounded; Mará Rose Williams, "Kansas Teen Uses 3-D Printer to Make Hand for Boy," *Kansas City Star*, January 31, 2014, www.kansascity.com/2014/01/31/3261314/kansas-teen-uses-3d-printer-to.html.
3. Michael Franco, "Giant 3D Printer Starts Spitting Out a House," CNET, March 14, 2014, www.cnet.com/news/giant-3D-printer-starts-spitting-out-a-house; Kathleen Miles, "This 3D Printer, Capable of Building a House in a Day, Could Change Construction Forever," Impact X, Huffington Post, January 21, 2014, www.huffingtonpost.com/2014/01/21/3D-printer-house-mars-slums_n_4639046.html.

Chapter 2

The Types of 3-D Printing

Abstract

Chapter 2 of Library Technology Reports *(vol. 50, no. 5) "3-D Printers for Libraries" describes in detail the predominant type of 3-D printing, fused deposition modeling (FDM). The chapter also covers stereolithography, selective laser sintering, and laminated object manufacturing.*

In chapter 1 I described the most common type of 3-D printing as a sort of robotic hot glue gun. This process, only one of multiple kinds of 3-D printing that are available, is usually referred to as *fused deposition modeling*. In this chapter we'll take a look at not only fused deposition modeling, but also selective laser sintering, stereolithography, laminated object manufacturing, and electron beam melting. While many of them are well outside the price point for most libraries, prices go down dramatically as soon as patents expire on the core technologies behind the printing methods. This is the central reason that fused deposition became inexpensive so quickly over the last five years, and most people that follow 3-D printing believe that laser sintering will follow suit shortly because a key patent for that technology expired in January 2014.

I'll start with the printing technology most central to libraries at the current time, fused deposition modeling, and then, after we wrap our heads around how that technology works, we'll take a look at other options that may be coming for us to use in the next three to five years.

Fused Deposition Modeling Printing

Fused deposition modeling (FDM) is what most people understand to be 3-D printing, as this technology is by far the most common and in many ways the simplest of the possibilities. FDM uses a variety of plastics that fall within a range of melting points and that fuse when melted and resolidified, the most common of which are ABS (acrylonitrile butadiene styrene) and PLA (polylactic acid). We'll discuss the specifics of these and other print substrates below.

The most common arrangement for an FDM printer is called a Cartesian print engine because it uses basic Cartesian coordinates (X, Y, Z) to create the printed objects. There are multiple types of printers even within this general category, although two are more common than others: the MakerBot style (see figure 2.1), which relies on a fixed plane X and Y printhead and movable Z print bed, and the so-called "RepRap" style, which relies on a fixed plane X axis, while the Y axis is controlled by moving the print bed itself and the Z axis is accomplished by moving the whole printhead system vertically upwards (see figure 2.2).

There is at least one other significantly different geometry for an FDM printer, the layout that is called a delta printer. In this instance, the printhead is suspended from three arms that are controlled along vertical supports while the print bed is completely stationary. This arrangement allows the printhead to "float" above the print bed and be located at any physical point in three dimensions simply by altering the relation of each of the three arms to the other. This is the same sort of control geometry at work in the flying cameras used in NFL games, applied to a robot. I will discuss two examples of a delta printer in chapter 5.

The Mechanics of Printing

Regardless of the control geometry used, the method of printing is the same for both types of FDM printers.

Figure 2.1
MakerBot Replicator

The printhead is a metal tube with a heating element and thermistor to control the temperature. The plastic substrate is melted by the heat of the printhead, and pressure is applied by forcing more plastic in, causing some of the liquid plastic to extrude through a small nozzle that ranges from .2 mm to .5 mm in size.

A print from an FDM printer begins with a single layer of plastic applied very thinly to the print bed, the nozzle moving across the print bed and depositing the plastic in the shape of the object it's creating. This initial layer is the base layer of the object, and the second layer will be deposited directly on top of the first and will fuse due to the properties of the plastic involved. Once the second layer is completed, the third, fourth, and so on will be done, building the object over time along the Z axis. You can think of layer height as the equivalent of the DPI (dots per inch) of a printed page. It's the resolution of the object in the vertical dimension, and the smaller the layer height, the smoother the final product will appear. It will also take significantly longer to print since as you reduce the layer height, you're adding layers to the overall build.

For example, let's imagine you're printing a 5-cm-tall cube. If you print that cube at what would be considered a fairly rough layer height of .3 mm, you'll print a total of 167 layers. If you print that same cube at a fine resolution (around .1 mm for most printers), then you'll print 500 layers, tripling the number of overall layers and the time necessary to print the object.

Because FDM printers rely on building objects vertically in the open air, they have issues with specific geometries of objects. If you imagine a thing being printed slowly from the bottom up, if the thing has a significant overhang or free-hanging part like a wide doorway or something like a stalactite, it won't be printable without supports on an FDM printer. The plastic has to be deposited on something: otherwise the print won't work.

All FDM printer software has the built-in ability to include supports for printing when issues like this arise. Printing an object with supports means that the software builds vertical towers whose only purpose is to give the object a structure upon which to print. In the best case, a support structure would be easily removable from the rest of the model, either by just peeling them apart or, in a slightly more advanced process, by printing the supports in a type of plastic that is soluble in a solvent, while printing the object itself in a plastic that is insoluble. The most popular of these support structures (discussed in more detail below) is high impact polystyrene, or HIPS, which allows a printer with dual extruders to print support structures that can be dissolved off the actual print.

Terminology

As with any sort of specialty product, there's a vocabulary that has built up around 3-D printing, and if you're new to looking at these printers, some of the specific terms are inscrutable without research. One example would be the terms for the two types of extruder setups found on FDM printers. The extruder is the part of the FDM printer that forces the plastic filament into the hot-end and through the nozzle onto the build plate. One is simply called a *direct extruder*, while the other is known as a *Bowden extruder*. On a direct extruder FDM printer, the moving print assembly includes the hot-end and the nozzle, and a motor pulls filament off the spool and drives it directly into the hot-end. The majority of FDM printers have a direct drive extruder. The Bowden extruder removes the motor assembly from the moving printhead. In a Bowden setup, the motor pushes the filament from the spool through a tube connected to the hot-end and nozzle. The advantage to the Bowden is that it significantly reduces the weight of the moving print assembly, which means that it can move more quickly and can change directions without serious jitter problems. The disadvantage is that it is, in some sense, pushing a rope, and the more flexible the filament is, the harder a time the Bowden setup will have with pushing it into the print assembly.

A few other helpful FDM-specific terms (and some of these I've already used without explaining, forgive me, dear reader) are *hot-end, build plate, nozzle*, and *spool*. The hot-end of an FDM printer is the metal piece

Figure 2.2
RepRap style 3-D printer. Photo credit: https://www.flickr.com/photos/jabella/8965235630 by John Abella

that contains the heating element and melts the filament when the filament reaches it. These are normally some form of nonreactive metal, either aluminum, brass, or stainless steel. The *nozzle* is the very small diameter (.2 mm to .5 mm) that the melted plastic is forced through under pressure on its way to the build plate. There is a relationship between the nozzle diameter and the possible layer height of the output from the printer. Because you are extruding tubes of melted plastic and they need to be pressed together in order to fuse, the layer height can't be any larger than the diameter of the nozzle. If it were, you would be extruding into thin air, without the new layer pressing into the old layer. To help visualize this, if the width of your extruded plastic is .3 mm and you attempt to print at a .4 mm layer height, there's .1 mm between the plastic and the layer below it—not good. In practice, a good rule of thumb is that the maximum layer height is somewhere between 75 and 80 percent of the nozzle diameter. So for a .4 mm diameter nozzle, your maximum layer height would be around .3 mm. Generally speaking, the goal is to have lower and lower print heights, as that makes for a smoother and smoother final product. But for rough prints, or demos, having a higher maximum layer height can speed up prints tremendously.

The last couple of FDM-specific pieces of terminology are *build plate* and *spool*. Spool is easy, as it's the way that filament is generally purchased and used. A typical purchase of ABS or PLA would be a kilogram (2.2 pounds) of plastic, wrapped onto a plastic or cardboard spool that hangs on the printer and plays out filament as needed. In an FDM printer, the build plate is the surface upon which the plastic is extruded. The specifics of the build plate vary widely but fall into a few basic categories, the primary of which is *heated* or *nonheated*. A heated build plate adds cost to the printer but is absolutely necessary for printing with certain types of filament (ABS, nylon, and others).

Another aspect of the build plate is what it's made of and whether you print directly onto the plate, onto some tape or other covering, or onto a glue or other adhesive. Heated build plates are usually made of either aluminum or tempered glass, although occasionally stainless steel shows up. Unheated build plates can be composed of the same things, as well as acrylic. The important thing with build plate construction is that you want something that will not warp or deform over time, since if the plate itself isn't flat, it's impossible to level it appropriately to the printheads. Glass is a very popular build plate material for this reason, although many FDM printers ship with aluminum plates that are then covered with a replaceable printing surface of some kind, most commonly PET tape or Kapton tape for a heated bed, or painter's tape for a nonheated bed.

Factors in Pricing

The price points for FDM printers are typically determined by size, more specifically print volume or the size of the print bed, and a variety of upgrades that make specific kinds of printing or printing with specific plastics more easily done. Print bed sizes range from very small (no more than 3 inches by 3 inches or so) to massive (over 12 inches by 12 inches). The print volume determines the maximum size of a single object that you can print or, conversely, the number of smaller objects that you can print at the same time. Printing larger objects is also more difficult because as you print larger things, there's more opportunity for a small error to creep into the print due any number of common 3-D printer issues.

Challenges with Fused Deposition Modeling

Most of the issues with FDM printing are related to the fact that it's a very mechanical process, and tuning the printer is key. The most sensitive aspect of the process is the relationship between the extruder/nozzle and the build plate. Because the printhead has to extrude an even layer of plastic onto the build plate, it's necessary that the build plate be perfectly flat relative to the nozzle. If there is any warp or unevenness, you'll get uneven attachment to the plate or other forms of print failure. This is the most common issue with FDM printing, especially with new operators. The first question that should always be asked if a print fails is, "Is my build plate level?"

And prints will fail. FDM printing is a complicated mechanical process, and while you can tune a FDM printer to be very reliable, at some point you will have a failure and will come back to a print that looks like someone poured plastic spaghetti on your build plate. This is normal. Recalibrate, relevel, and try again.

Stereolithography

While FDM printing is by far the most common inexpensive method of 3-D printing, we are starting to see stereolithography (SLA) printing move down-market into the affordable-for-libraries zone. I'm aware of a couple of libraries that have already purchased stereolithography printers, so it is starting to trickle into our midst. What is stereolithography? It's a method of 3-D printing that involves a light-sensitive resin and lasers. A liquid resin is contained in the body of the printer, with a build plate that moves up and down inside the resin. The resin solidifies when exposed to a specific wavelength of light, usually in the UV spectrum, and the printer has a laser or lasers that are tuned to that specific wavelength. The build plate starts near the top of the resin, and the lasers sweep across, solidifying the resin in the appropriate areas. The build plate then lowers, and the lasers repeat their sweep, building layer after layer, one after the other, as the object is built. You can also have this process occur upside down, as in the Formlabs Form 1 printer, where the build plate is actually above the resin, and as layers are added, it pulls the completed layer out of the resin.

This type of printing has several advantages over FDM printing. First, because the print is always encased in liquid resin as it prints, it is much more forgiving as to geometry of design. Not completely, as there still has to be some connection to the base layer (you couldn't print a "floating" horizontal piece, for instance). But in general, the resin provides substantially more support for designs than you are capable of printing with FDM printers. The other major advantage is that the detail level is limited by the crystallization of the liquid and the size of the lasers, which means that you can have very, very fine details in an SLA print. It's possible to achieve .025 mm (25 microns) layer heights with SLA prints.

Stereolithography printing is limited in some ways as well. The first is that the resin is available only in a very limited number of colors, generally clear or translucent and white. When compared to the rainbow of colors available for FDM printing with ABS or PLA, it feels limiting. The second, and far more worrisome, limitation is that most vendors of this type of printer manufacture their own resin, and it's possible to tune the wavelength of the lasers involved to the specific resin they sell, thus making it very difficult for anyone to compete with them on consumables for the printer. This would be the equivalent of buying a printer from HP and having to then buy paper and toner from HP as well in order to use the printer.

Small SLA printers are just beginning to hit the market, available in the $2,500 to $3,500 range. The consumable for printing, the photosensitive resin, is more expensive than filament for FDM printing, too. The most popular of consumer-grade SLA printers, the Formlabs Form 1, has resin that sells for $149 per liter.

Selective Laser Sintering

Simultaneously, the most flexible and the most expensive type of 3-D printing commonly used, selective laser sintering (SLS), is similar to stereolithography in that it uses lasers to solidify a loose substrate. But in SLS the printing substrate is a powder and you use high-energy lasers rather than UV ones. The high-energy lasers selectively fuse sections of a powder together, a new layer of powder is deposited on top of the sintered layer as the entire print bed drops, and the lasers do another pass, fusing the single layer of powder to the already solid layer below. Thus prints are completed layer by layer, exactly as in the other printing technologies that we have covered, except the end product is a solid object that's been drawn by lasers, encased in all of the powder that wasn't fused.

This method provides total support for the print in question, so nearly any imaginable geometry can be printed using SLS printing. It is also possible to use any material for SLS that is capable of being powdered and fused with heat, including most of the previously mentioned thermoplastics as well as steel, aluminum, titanium, and other metals and alloys. Prints produced in this way are very nearly as strong as solid-cast parts, which means that it's possible via SLS printing to 3-D print mechanical parts that are directly usable in engineering projects.

Layer height and resolution in SLS printing are completely determined by the resolution of the powder being fused, but they are typically on par with

SLA printing, averaging around .1 mm layer heights. Another similar technology is electron beam melting (EBM), which uses high-energy electron beams to melt powdered metals in order to produce 3-D objects. The use of electron beams allows for even higher precision than lasers, as small as .05 mm layer heights, which is nearly unheard of by any other method.

Laminated Object Manufacturing

The last specific type of 3-D printing that I'd like to describe is, in my opinion, particularly clever. Laminated object manufacturing takes thin materials like paper or plastic sheets, cuts them to a specific shape, and then uses adhesive to glue one layer to the next. The best known of these types of printers is manufactured by a company called Mcor Technologies. Its printer uses normal, ordinary copy paper as its substrate, cutting one sheet at a time into the appropriate shape for the given layer and then using paper glue to laminate the individual layers together. The high-end Mcor printer includes a full-color ink-jet printhead inside to allow the creation of full-color 3-D prints from very inexpensive raw materials—literally paper, ink, and glue.

Other 3-D Printing Types

There are numerous other 3-D printing technologies in existence, especially those that are patented and limited to a single company. For example, 3D Systems uses a type of 3-D printing methodology it calls Color-Jet Printing (CJP), which uses two different materials that are combined using a sort of high-end ink-jet printer in order to create the solid end product. This patented process allows 3D Systems to print in materials like food-grade ceramic. 3D Systems also makes a 3-D printer that is capable of printing in sugar, called the ChefJet, and the high-end model, the ChefJet Pro, can print edible 3-D models in full color.

Chapter 3

Types of Plastics

Abstract

Chapter 3 of Library Technology Reports *(vol. 50, no. 5) "3-D Printers for Libraries" covers the two major types of filaments used in 3-D printing, ABS and PLA. The chapter also covers in brief several other less common plastics.*

The substrate for FDM printers is almost exclusively some form of thermoplastic that is delivered in an extruded wire-like form on a spool and is usually called "filament" in the generic. The two common diameters for use in FDM printing are 1.75 mm and 3 mm, and a specific diameter is called for by the printhead being used for the printer in question. A printer that uses 1.75 mm diameter filament won't be able to use 3 mm without retrofitting the hardware for the difference, and vice versa. The 1.75 mm size is slightly more commonly used and is the filament diameter used by the most popular manufacturer of FDM printers, MakerBot Industries.

As I talk in chapter 5 about the different printer types and manufacturers, I'll make a point of mentioning what type of filament they can print because that turns out to be a major limitation and will affect any purchasing decision.

ABS

The original fused deposition printers almost exclusively used ABS (acrylonitrile butadiene styrene) as their substrate for printing. ABS has nearly ideal properties for rapid prototyping in plastic: it's a strong, slightly flexible plastic that extrudes cleanly at between 220° and 240° Celsius. ABS is used in Lego bricks and is one of the most commonly used industrial and commercial plastics.

For FDM printing, ABS requires a heated print bed to ease the thermal shock. Heating the print build plate helps the plastic adhere to the plate for stability and prevents it cooling too quickly, which could lead to thermal deformation (a sort of curling or separation when ABS cools rapidly after being extruded). ABS is sensitive enough in this arena that many people who print ABS learned early on that enclosing the printer would increase the stability of prints because it regulated the temperature around the printer. I discovered early in my printing experiments with an early MakerBot printer (Replicator 1) that even a strong breeze blowing in the wrong place (i.e., across the print bed) could wreak havoc with getting a good print out of the printer. Higher-end printers will have an enclosed print area built in, while less expensive ones won't.

One of the advantages of ABS is that it dissolves in acetone. Acetone dissolves ABS completely, but used sparingly it can act as a glue to fuse two ABS printed pieces together permanently. Acetone is also used to make a "glue" for print beds to make them sticky for the initial printed layers. Acetone vapor is heavier than air, and some people have used this property to build acetone vapor baths that act to smooth the edges of layers of an FDM ABS print.

ABS has caught some bad press recently as the potential effects of off-gassing of the heated plastic and microparticulate effects are studied. As a petroleum-based plastic, ABS does produce a distinctive stink when printing. Fumes have been reported to cause headaches, and some studies link ABS fumes to olfactory loss.[1] One study found ABS printing releases high volumes of ultrafine particles that could be dangerous when inhaled.[2] These are preliminary studies.

Most haven't been repeated, and the science is still rough on the health effects. But if you need to print with ABS, it may be a good idea to take venting into account.

PLA

PLA (polylactic acid) is the second-most popular printing substrate for FDM printers. PLA is a bioplastic, made from corn, beets, or potatoes, and is compostable in commercial compost facilities (the heat and bacterial action in home composting aren't high enough to break it down). It melts at a much lower temperature than ABS (150–160°C), but it is typically extruded at a higher temperature, anywhere from 180°C to 220°C depending on the PLA itself. Because of its lower temperature, it's not suitable for uses that involve high temperatures and direct sunlight. PLA is also very different from ABS in term of fragility; PLA is far more crystalline and shatters or cracks more readily than ABS, rather than deforming under pressure.

However, MakerBot and other major manufacturers are now starting to go with PLA as their primary printing plastic. PLA doesn't require a heated bed to promote adhesion or prevent thermal curling, which lowers the price of the printers that use it. It's far more thermally stable during printing than ABS as well, and much less likely to warp or curl due to errant breezes. It is possible to reliably print PLA without needing to enclose your printer, which can be a huge benefit in many circumstances.

The other significant advantage is that PLA is far more pleasant when printing than ABS. Because it is a bioplastic, when heated it smells like waffles or syrup and not like an oil spill. It also hasn't been linked to any type of medical issues from being heated, although the study of all these plastics is young when it comes to 3-D printing specifically.

One of the other advantages of PLA is that it's available in dozens and dozens of colors, including both opaque and partially transparent, as well as a couple of glow-in-the-dark colors. It also is available in a flexible form, which can produce prints that are almost rubber-like in consistency.

If you are printing in a library setting, I would suggest concentrating on using PLA. Between reliability and ease of working with it, it's a far better choice than ABS for printing in a public space.

Other Plastics

Once you get beyond ABS and PLA, you're in the realm of specialized plastics that are used for specific properties rather than for general 3-D printing. There are more and more of these practically every day, but generally they fall into a couple of categories: dissolvable support material, specific required material qualities, or nonplastic powder suspended in a thermoplastic resin. I'll describe the most common of these below.

HIPS

High impact polystyrene, or HIPS, is a plastic filament used for dissolvable support structures in FDM printers. It extrudes at around 235°C, and its material properties are very similar to ABS. The main difference is that HIPS is completely soluble in a liquid hydrocarbon called limonene. This means that if you have an FDM printer with more than one printhead, you can extrude ABS from one and HIPS as a support material from the other. If you sit the final printed model in a bath of limonene, the HIPS will dissolve away, leaving only the ABS behind, thus allowing for nearly impossible geometries to be printed, including moving ball bearings and more.

Nylon

There are at least four types of nylon currently available for use in FDM printers: Nylon 618, Nylon 645, Nylon 680, and Nylon 910. These vary in their color from medium transparency to fully opaque white, and all are extraordinarily strong compared to other FDM substrates. They are also very resistant to solvents and such, although they are dyeable with acid-based dyes.

Nylon is more expensive than PLA or ABS. The major reason for using nylon would be for specific material properties (resistance to specific chemicals) or because of the need for FDA-approved materials, as both Nylon 680 and 910 are undergoing FDA approval for use, something rare in the 3-D printer world.

T-Glase

T-Glase is a brand name for a filament composed of polyethylene terephthalate. Of all 3-D printer filaments, it is the most glasslike. Nearly transparent, especially at small sizes, it could easily be mistaken for glass. At larger sizes, it is still very light-transmissive, if not fully transparent. T-Glase prints at around 221°C on a heated bed, but it is very stable and resistant to curling.

LayBrick and LayWood

LayBrick and LayWood, another type of printing material for FDM printers, fall squarely in the experimental realm. They are made by a single manufacturer and are both a sort of hybrid filament, with a powdered material being supported inside a resin. In the case of LayWood, fine wood particles are suspended in a thermoplastic resin; in the case of LayBrick, very finely crushed chalk and other minerals are suspended in the resin.

Both LayBrick and LayWood have the interesting property of variability in appearance depending on the temperature at which they are printed. LayBrick can range from a very smooth, almost ceramic feel to very rough sandstone when the heat of extrusion is increased. For very smooth, you print at a low temperature (165–190°C); going up from there to around 210°C will render the printed part rougher and rougher. For LayWood, the difference is in the appearance of the final product. By increasing the temperature, you get darker and darker wood grain from the output, so you can actually vary the look from light to dark wood (or, if you have a printer that supports variable temperatures during a single print, you can get different colors in a single print by varying the temperature).

One of the risks, however, with both of these is that the filament isn't uniform in construction, which means that it's possible to clog your extruder if the nozzle opening is smaller than the particulate in the filament itself. FDM printer nozzle openings range from .35 mm to .5 mm, and on the lower end of that, especially with LayWood, you risk clogging a nozzle (it is harder to ensure regular sizes with organic particles than with inorganic particulate). I know 3-D printers that have clogged even at .4 mm nozzle using LayWood; for printing these sorts of filaments, the larger the nozzle the better.

Polypropylene

Still very experimental, polypropylene (PP) offers the possibility of food-grade 3-D prints. Polypropylene should work with any FDM printer at an extrusion temperature of 210°C and a heated print bed set to 90°C. It looks like PP is really available only in black.

Notes

1. Shu-Fang Cheng, Mei-Lien Chen, Po-Chen Hung, Chiou-Jong Chen, and I-Fang Mao, "Olfactory Loss in Poly (Acrylonitrile-Butadiene-Styrene) Plastic Injection-Moulding Workers," *Occupational Medicine* 54, no. 7 (October 2004): 469–74, available on PubMed.gov, www.ncbi.nlm.nih.gov/pubmed/15486179.
2. Brent Stephens, Parham Azimi, Zeineb El Orch, and Tiffanie Ramos, "Ultrafine Partile Emissions from Desktop 3D Printers," *Atmospheric Environment* 79 (November 2013): 334–39, doi:10.1016/j.atmosenv.2013.06.050.

Chapter 4

Creating and Printing Files

Abstract

Chapter 4 of Library Technology Reports *(vol. 50, no. 5) "3-D Printers for Libraries" covers software for use with 3-D printing. After introducing the two common file formats and a sharing site for files, the chapter covers three software packages for design, organized by the level of expertise they require. The chapter also covers products that scan physical objects and the operational software that interfaces between a file and the 3-D printer's mechanisms.*

Before we get into the software proper, a high-level overview of the process of printing with an FDM printer will be helpful. This is a generic description of process, but regardless of which particular printer you have, the process will be very similar. You start with a digital model in STL format. You've either created it yourself using one of the software packages described below or downloaded it from a website; either way, you have an STL that you'd like to print. You take that file and open it in a plating and slicing program, like MakerWare, Repetier-Host, ReplicatorG, or Pronterface. That program will let you see how the object sits on the build platform and manipulate it to some degree (scale it up or down, rotate it for a better fit). You will then choose a number of different settings for slicing, things like layer height, infill, and extrusion temperature. Once you have your settings, you will either print directly from the computer over USB or export the STL file as a G-code file and move it to the printer on an SD card. The STL will be sliced into hundreds of layers, and the 3-D printer will be given instructions on how to build it one layer at a time.

Now that we have an understanding of the physical process by which 3-D printers work, let's look at the other half of the 3-D printing process: the software.

There are two different sorts of software we'll discuss in this chapter: the software that prepares your designed files for printing (slicing and plating software) and the actual design software that allows you to create the 3-D object that you wish to print.

File Formats

There are a couple of different filetype standards for 3-D printing, STL and OBJ. OBJ files are typically those used in high-end printing and include things, like color information, that are superfluous for the sorts of consumer-level printing that libraries are likely to be involved in. For FDM and STL printing the needed output file is an STL file. This is the equivalent of needing a .docx file if you want to work in the most recent version of Word or a PDF file for cross-platform document consumption. The STL file is a very simple description, in either ASCII or binary, of the external shell of a 3-D object in terms of triangles. Nearly every 3-D modeling software that you might use will export to STL—it is that common a file format in 3-D design.

One of the things that has really helped the 3-D printing business take off is the availability of freely shareable STL models of just about anything you can think up. The most popular online library of 3-D models is Thingiverse, a freely available resource that is owned by MakerBot Industries. Thingiverse allows anyone who has created a 3-D model to upload it to the website and make it available for anyone else to download. It's open-access 3-D objects, in effect. Thingiverse is the perfect first stop for anyone who has a 3-D printer, as it will give you hundreds of things to print, from toys to tools. The downloadable files have easy-to-follow instructions for printing if there is anything tricky about the print and clearly labeled intellectual property rights that make it easy to understand what you can do with the design itself.

As libraries start creating and sharing more of their own objects, Thingiverse would be the logical place to store them, especially for findability by the 3-D community. I'm hopeful that we'll be able to find shelf brackets and more that are printable and shareable over time.

Thingiverse
www.thingiverse.com

Design Software

I'm going to organize this recommendation area for 3-D design software into beginner, intermediate, and expert levels. There are far more options for design software than I can cover here, but this section is designed to give you a solid starting point. I will also point out a couple of options for the creation of STL files from photographs.

Beginning

My favorite piece of software for the beginner in 3-D design is a website called Tinkercad. Tinkercad is a freely available web application that allows the creation of 3-D models by using simple shapes to build up more complicated ones. It does require the creation of an account, but the free account (at least at the current time) gives you unlimited models online, and the only real limitation is that the free account requires that your creations be Creative Commons Attribution-Share Alike 3.0 license. Paid accounts get the ability to choose among all of the available Creative Commons licenses as well as the ability to control commercial distribution of their models.

Since Tinkercad is entirely browser-based and runs on any modern web browser, it's trivial to run on nearly any computer. It has a well-done introductory tutorial for beginners and works by building with simple basic shapes (cube, sphere, pyramid), allowing people who are new to 3-D modeling to start very slowly but still gain understanding of basic concepts. It also clearly labels the size of objects for output and allows either solids or holes of any arbitrary shape.

Tinkercad also allows the importing of other STL files, which means that it's possible to download an STL from Thingiverse, import it into Tinkercad, and alter or modify it, although not in the robust way that you could in a full 3-D modeling software. As first steps towards creativity in the 3-D realm, it's a fantastic tool.

Very similar to Tinkercad, and also browser-based, is 3DTin. I find it less intuitive than Tinkercad, but it has some tools (camera movement, for example) that might make it a useful answer for a problem you have in 3-D creation.

Tinkercad
https://www.tinkercad.com

3DTin
www.3Dtin.com

Intermediate

A step up from Tinkercad is SketchUp, a piece of software that was formerly owned by Google but sold off in 2012 to Trimble Navigation. There are two versions of SketchUp available, SketchUp Make and SketchUp Pro. SketchUp Make is freely available for noncommercial use and has every capability that I can imagine a library or patron needing, while SketchUp Pro is really designed for professional architects and others who need professional-level controls and output.

SketchUp is ostensibly designed for architectural renderings, building interiors and exteriors, landscape design—that sort of thing. But since, like Tinkercad, it deals in just a few basic shapes and controls, it's very flexible with what can be designed with it. As a bonus, the SketchUp website has dozens of learning resources that you can use to both learn and help other people learn the tool.

SketchUp doesn't natively have the ability to export to STL for 3-D printing, but there is an easily installed plugin that gives it the ability to export or import any STL file. This can come in particularly handy if you are interested in printing buildings, as SketchUp is the primary tool used for creation of buildings for Google Earth and Google Maps. SketchUp maintains a 3-D warehouse of buildings and objects that can be trivially opened and printed, including pretty much every famous building or sculpture in the world. Want a copy of the Taj Mahal on your desk? No problem with SketchUp and a 3-D printer. Ditto for the Empire State Building, the Arc de Triomphe, or the Tennessee Aquarium. All of those are available and already modeled for your use.

SketchUp
www.sketchup.com

Advanced

Another of the free tools that I want to mention is Blender. Blender is an open-source 3-D computer graphics program that is used not only for basic 3-D model creation but also for full animation and movie

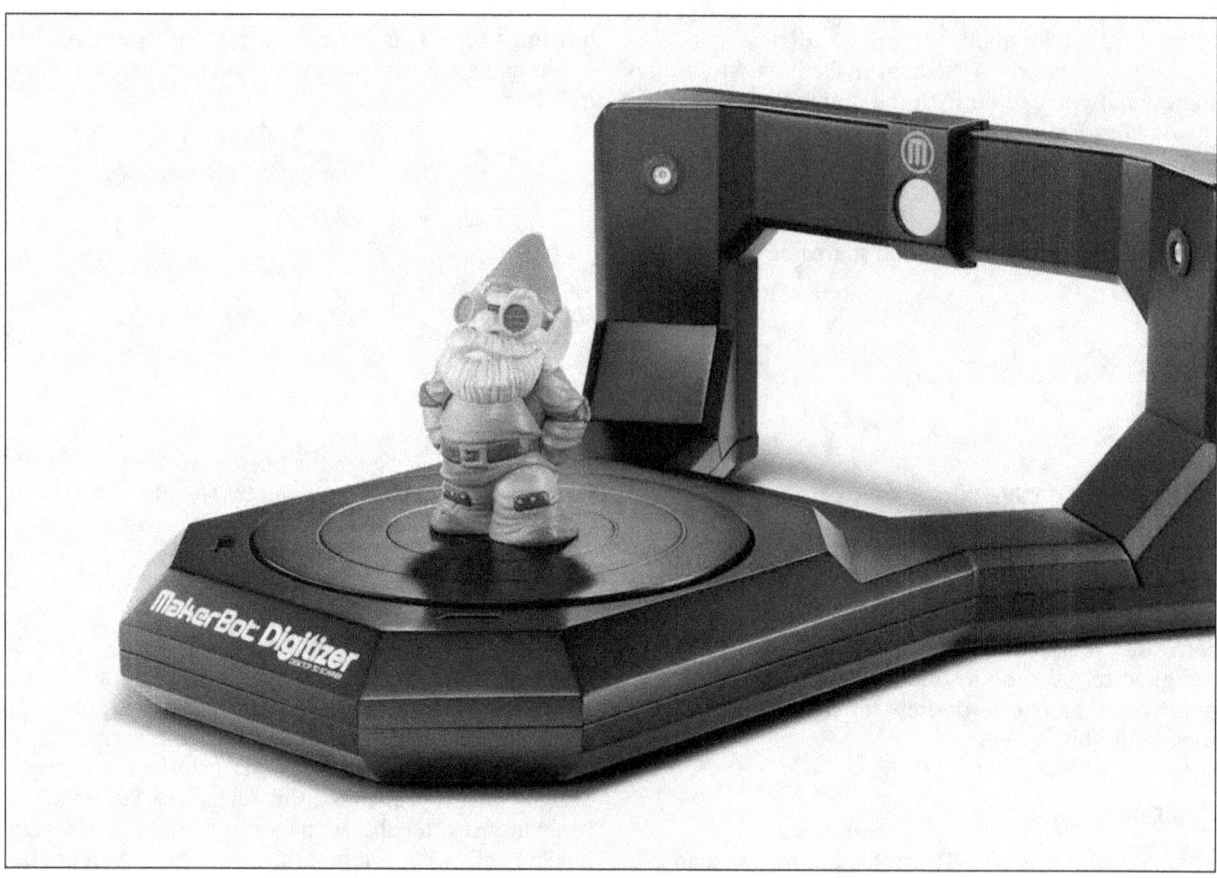

Figure 4.1
MakerBot Digitizer

making. In the software that I've mentioned, if Tinkercad is a moped and SketchUp is a motorcycle, Blender is a Saturn V rocket. It is indescribably more complex than either of the other tools, to such a degree that I would really recommend it only for people who have previous experience with professional-level 3-D tools.

With that caveat, it is a fully professional-level tool that is capable of creating completely realized 3-D photorealistic models. And it's free. This combination means that there's little reason not to at least play with it or have it available if a patron wants to use it. It is worth considering whether or not you will be able to offer assistance to your patrons in using Blender because, for most libraries, the answer would be no. This is, I think, not a bad thing, but you should be aware of the complexity of the program.

The last of the free tools I'd like to suggest taking a look at is OpenSCAD, an open-source CAD editor. It is also a professional tool, but where Blender's strength is in the artistic and creative, OpenSCAD's strength is in the mechanical and engineering aspects of 3-D modeling. If you want to model a turbine impeller or a structural support, OpenSCAD is likely your tool. Much like Blender, however, it is definitively a professional tool and requires serious research and effort to get into.

Most of the commercial tools for 3-D model creation are tied heavily to specific professions, and it's likely that if your library needs them, you'll already know it because of local demand. Academic libraries specifically may need to pay close attention to the areas they are serving, as classes that use AutoCAD (for architecture, engineering, and construction) are very unlikely to also teach Maya (for 3-D animation), but either may be very important to your patrons.

Blender
www.blender.org

OpenSCAD
www.openscad.org

3-D Scanning

In addition to printing "born digital" objects, it is possible to digitize existing real-world objects in such a way that they can be printed. This is usually just called 3-D scanning, and there are a variety of ways this can

Figure 4.2
3D Systems Sense

be done. I'll mention my favorite three possibilities, although much like 3-D printing, the technology for scanning is changing quickly.

3-D scanning is still a rough art in that no capture method reproduces exactly the object that is being scanned. Some types of scanning technology have issues with the separation of background from object, and even things like going from a very dark to a very light surface can cause problems. Most 3-D scans will require some finessing in order to get very good results from the resultant print. With just a bit of work, though, you can get really interesting and useful things from a scanner.

MakerBot Digitizer

MakerBot Industries has released a desktop 3-D scanner called the Digitizer (see figure 4.1). It's roughly the size of a turntable and can scan objects up to 8 inches in diameter. It uses a camera and lasers to "draw" the edges of an object as it is slowly turned around a single point. The Digitizer is also linked to the MakerBot Desktop software, and if you have a MakerBot printer, you can have the Digitizer and the Replicator together act like a copy machine, placing an object on the Digitizer platform and then having it feed directly to the Replicator.

The Digitizer is limited in that it collects only volumetric information and can't capture surface colors. Other scanners can, and while the most common FDM printers available now can't do full color, higher-end printers can, and it may be that scanning things and expecting them to be archival quality will change as the scanners get better. The Digitizer now sells for $799.

3D Systems Sense

The Sense by 3D Systems (see figure 4.2) is a handheld scanner that uses proprietary methods (which include at least camera and IR sensors) to create 3-D scans of objects from 8 inches to 118 inches. It's a far more interesting and overall more powerful scanner than the Digitizer in that it allows you to scan absolutely arbitrary objects rather than being limited to things that will fit onto a turntable. You can scan freestanding objects, people, parts of rooms—nearly anything.

The software for the system originally ran only on Windows PCs, but the company recently released a version for Macintosh systems. It also showed off a version of the Sense that worked with the iPad at CES 2014, which would be an excellent and truly portable solution.

The other thing that the Sense has going for it is price. It's only $399 for the basic Sense unit, and for the power that it affords you, it's a very good deal.

123D Catch

The last of the 3-D scanning gadgets that I wanted to mention actually isn't a gadget at all. 123D Catch is one of the coolest options for capturing a physical object. The software- and app-based option uses standard photographs to recreate objects through the use of very clever and complicated math. You simply take a series of photos around the object, changing the position each time, until you circumscribe the object in roughly 15 degree arcs. The software then interpolates the object from the photos, using the shadows and highlights to get depth from the series of photos.

123D Catch is available in three forms: a universal iOS app that allows you to take pics in the app itself, a Windows app that allows you to load photos into it directly from another source (a DSLR or other digital camera), or as a web app that does many of the same things as the PC app, allowing you to upload photos taken elsewhere and convert them to a 3-D model.

All of these are free to use, in limited ways. The iOS app is only for noncommercial uses of the models, but as a freely available service, it's really borderline magic what 123D Catch can do with static 2-D photographs. The key advantage of the Catch is that you can use it in places where people would look at you oddly if you brought in a dedicated 3-D scanner but don't blink if you take a series of photographs. Think about 123D Catch at next museum or art gallery you visit, take a few extra shots, and give it a try.

3-D Scanning

MakerBot Digitizer
http://store.makerbot.com/digitizer

3D Systems Sense
http://cubify.com/en/Products/Sense

123D Catch
www.123dapp.com/catch

Operational Software

What I'm calling operational software is the software that you use to interface with the 3-D printer directly, whether it's preparing STL files for printing or actually creating the output file that the printer understands.

This section is going to focus on the software needed for FDM printing, as that's the most likely to be of use in a library (and once you get into SLS and other types, it's more likely that the software and process are proprietary).

Much like a desktop printer doesn't speak Microsoft Word, even if that is the most common filetype that you print, 3-D printers don't actually print STL files. An STL is a mathematical representation of a shape, while the 3-D printer itself needs instructions: how much filament to extrude, where and how fast to move the nozzle, how far and when to lower the build platform, how hot the extruder should be. The actual mechanical movements are encoded in a separate file, and the filetype depends on the printer in question. Most FDM printers use an open filetype called a G-code file that is normally an ASCII representation of all of the values needed to create the object. ASCII G-code is very handy, in that since it's just a text file, you can manually alter known values in order to change the way the print is done. If you want to lower the extrusion temperature, no need to re-encode the file: you can literally just change the value once you know where it is. G-code is also an open file format, which means there are multiple programs that can create it.

The process of moving from STL file to G-code for 3-D printing is called "slicing" because you are in effect taking the 3-D object and slicing it into thin layers that the printer will reproduce. Some slicing software has a ton of control, letting you "plate" the models. Plating means to place them on a virtual representation of the build plate of the printer in question, allowing for printing of multiple parts simultaneously by plating more than one STL at the same time. Other slicing software is more bare bones, allowing you to make choices as to printer settings during the print process.

Slic3r

The most popular slicing engine is called, appropriately enough, Slic3r. Slic3r is an open-source project that is usable by itself but is probably more commonly used as backend slicing software for more popular packages that include plating and other options. These would include MatterControl, Pronterface, ReplicatorG, and Repetier-Host, the most popular management software for 3-D printers. Slic3r does allow for rough plating of objects, but its strength is in the detail given to the slicing process.

Slicr3r has three main areas of control: print settings, filament settings, and printer settings. Each can be saved independently of the others, allowing for a collection of presets to be designed around your most common printing needs. The simplest of these areas is the printer setup, which allows you to set the size of the printer build platform, as well as details about the extruder. Generally speaking, you just need one printer setup for each printer that you want to use with Slic3r. The filament settings are also not likely to change very much, as Slic3r allows you to set just the diameter of your filament and the desired printing temperature for the extruder and bed. The real power comes from the print settings, where you have almost total control over every other aspect of the behavior of the print. Under print settings, you'll find options for layer height, infill, speed, skirt and brim, support, and more.

We've discussed layer height, but the other settings are likely to be a bit mysterious. *Infill* controls the solidity of the print, the amount of material used to fill the interior, expressed as a percentage. The software does the math and determines how to arrange the type of infill you choose (square, hexagonal, etc.) in order to achieve the correct percentage of infill. As an example, if we were printing a 200 mm cube, and wanted it to be totally hollow, we would set the infill to 0. Setting the infill to a very low percentage—between 1 percent and 10 percent or so—would result in very large square or hexagonal infill on each layer, and as you increased the percentage, the infill would become denser and denser, until at 100 percent infill, you would get a solid piece of plastic. You would almost never print an object at 100 percent infill, as there is a diminishing return for increasing the infill as it relates to strength versus the amount of plastic used. Over 60 to 70 percent or so, you'll likely not find any actual structural advantage unless there's a very specific geometry that needs to be solid. I find myself printing most things at under a 20 percent infill as a sweet spot of strength and weight to amount of plastic (and thus cost to print).

Speed is the speed at which the printhead moves around the build plate. FDM printing is a slow effort, and one way to speed up the process is just to make the printhead move faster as it's depositing the plastic. There are issues with simply cranking the speed up, though. As you increase the speed, there is a point at which you will begin to decrease the quality of the output. There's a limit as to how fast you can move and extrude plastic cleanly, and each printer has a sweet spot of speed that produces great-looking prints as quickly as possible. The other issue that arises is that the printheads on these printers are fairly heavy, with motors and metal heat sinks and brass nozzles. As you begin to move this not insubstantial mass faster and faster, you create a significant amount of inertia that can be more than the printer body can contain. There are videos online of printers "walking" across a desk as the printhead is thrown back and forth across the build plate.

The last part of the print settings that you want to pay particular attention to is the support material settings. These include both raft settings and support settings. A *raft* is a thin (two to three layers) platform of plastic that can be printed as a sort of buffer between the build plate and the print itself. For certain prints, this can help with adhesion and curl issues. *Supports* are the other bit that are important in this section. Supports, as previously mentioned, are vertical structures built not as a part of the model but as a method of supporting an overhang in the model, giving the printer a base layer upon which to print the overhang in question. You can choose whether or not to have supports and the shape they take.

Once you get all of these settings tuned for your particular printer, you would need to change very few from print to print. Slic3r supports saving profiles, so you could do a series of printer settings for the slight variations that you might do most often, like 10 percent infill, 25 percent infill, etc. Or if you do print with multiple filament types, you could have one profile for PLA and another for ABS, with all of the appropriate temperature changes and such presets.

Slic3r works with any 3-D fused deposition printer that speaks G-code, which is the vast majority of the printers. The bad news is that the most popular 3-D printer for libraries doesn't use G-code, isn't compatible with Slic3r, and instead uses a proprietary piece of software and slicing filetype. I'm talking, of course, about MakerBot and MakerWare.

MakerWare and MakerBot Desktop

MakerBot is the company with by far the most popular consumer 3-D printer on the market today. It has likely sold more FDM printers to consumers than all other printer manufacturers combined, and it has chosen to go its own way when it comes to software to run the printers. MakerBot printers made prior to this year use software called MakerWare to manage their printing, and it's a far more user-friendly process than I've described for Slic3r above. The newest MakerBot printers (their 5th Generation printers) are designed to use an even more powerful piece of software, MakerBot Desktop. We'll talk a little about both below, although Desktop is still heavily in beta.

MakerWare is an all-in-one MakerBot management tool. It will take one or more STL files, allow you to place them on the build platform, rotate, scale, and otherwise manipulate them, and then set all of your printer specifics before hitting Print. It's very visual, easy to use, and designed for first-use 3-D printing. If you have a MakerBot model with multiple extruders, it also allows you to set the specifics of each extruder and designate which parts on the build platform get built in the respective plastics.

MakerWare also has the ability to output a printable file that can be moved to the printer on an SD card, although MakerBot doesn't use the standard G-code format that most other 3-D printers use. It has its own proprietary file format (x3g) that isn't compatible with other printers. You can also print directly to a compatible MakerBot printer that is connected by USB, although most people with experience recommend printing from the SD card rather than live from computer. This is because it eliminates the problems that may come if there is an issue with the computer, like a reboot or a program crash. If you print directly from SD, it eliminates that possibility.

MakerWare is compatible with all of the MakerBot printers prior to the 5th Generation (the Replicator, Replicator 2, and Replicator 2x).

MakerBot Desktop is the newest 3-D printer software for controlling MakerBot 5th Generation printers. Those are the Replicator Mini, the Replicator (5th Generation), and the Replicator Z18. They require a different piece of software because they've added a lot of hardware features not found on other 3-D printers, including built-in webcams, Wi-Fi accessibility, "smart" extruders, and more.

While the interface for MakerBot Desktop is slightly different, the basic functionality is the same as MakerWare. You can import, position, rotate, and plate STL files to prep them for output. But that's the least of its features, as it also includes access to the new MakerBot Cloud service, allowing you to maintain a library of 3-D designs in the cloud and access them from any computer running MakerBot Desktop simply by logging in. MakerBot has also introduced yet another filetype, the .makerbot file, which is used as the printable output file for the 5th Generation printers.

The addition of cameras in each of the new MakerBot printers also enables MakerBot Desktop to be a visual monitor of your prints regardless of where you are. You are able to view the printing locally or remotely and control the printer remotely, including pausing or canceling prints. You can even use it to snap pics for uploading your model to Thingiverse.

For libraries, the biggest impact might be felt by use of one of the smallest actual feature additions to MakerBot Desktop. When you plate an STL file in MakerBot Desktop, it can give you both a time-to-print estimate and a total amount of plastic used, both of which are almost impossible to determine before you print on pretty much any other platform.

Chapter 5

3-D Printers

Abstract

Chapter 5 of Library Technology Reports *(vol. 50, no. 5) "3-D Printers for Libraries" provides detailed descriptions of the most popular printers for libraries. Author Jason Griffey offers general buying advice by comparing features to anticipated library uses.*

In this chapter I'm going to list and discuss the 3-D printers that are available and meet a few criteria. I'm not going to try to be a completist in my listing, because even at this point it would be nearly impossible to find all of the different 3-D printers on the market. By the time this Report actually gets to print, it will be further out of date. So I'm going to talk about the most popular printers in detail, while mentioning and differentiating between a number of others. I will try to give buying advice for libraries, taking into account the possible differences in use case that they may have. I'll also be talking about support, something that could be make-or-break for implementation, especially in small libraries.

In the places I talk about build plate area, all of the numbers will be listed as length (the X axis, or side-to-side in the printer) by width (the Y axis, or back-to-front in the printer) by height (the Z axis, or print height).

MakerBot

As mentioned previously, the 800-pound gorilla in the consumer 3-D printer market is MakerBot Industries. MakerBot was founded in 2009 and began its life as a member of the RepRap community, a 3-D printer community that started in 2005 in an attempt to make a 3-D printer that could replicate itself. MakerBot Industries has had two very different periods in the philosophy and design of its 3-D printers: the open-source period (Cupcake through Replicator) and the closed-source period (Replicator 2 through current models).

The first printer made and sold by MakerBot was the Cupcake CNC, so named because that was roughly the size of the objects it would output. MakerBot quickly iterated on the Cupcake, improving it and releasing the Thing-O-Matic in 2010, which brought with it a better extruder design, heated bed, and larger build volume. Both of these printers were sold as kits, with the expectation that users would put significant time into building the printer themselves. The last of the printers MakerBot made and sold in its open-source period was the Replicator, a radical new design that added significantly to the build volume available as well as being available as a prebuilt unit. As one of the first out-of-the-box 3-D printers, the Replicator was a huge success.

The Cupcake, Thing-O-Matic, and Replicator were all designed around printing with ABS filament, although all were capable of printing with PLA as well. They all use 1.75 mm filament. The Replicator also was one of the first consumer devices to provide dual-extrusion capabilities.

With the release of the Replicator 2 in 2012, MakerBot turned the corner away from open-source designs and started to produce printers with closed aspects. The Replicator 2 schematics and circuit board diagrams were not available, and it was at this point that MakerBot switched from the open standard for G-code to its own proprietary standard of x3g files. The Replicator 2 was designed specifically for printing in PLA, with no heated build platform. For those

Figure 5.1
The MakerBot Replicator (5th Generation), Replicator Mini, and Replicator Z18

interested in printing in ABS, MakerBot released a version of the Replicator 2 that it simply called the Replicator 2X. It had a heated print bed and dual extruders that allowed for printing of two different types of filament simultaneously. Both of these were very successful for MakerBot, and while I don't have hard numbers, I would bet that the majority of 3-D printers currently installed in libraries are models of the MakerBot Replicator 2.

In 2014, MakerBot released a brand-new version of its Replicator line, called simply the Replicator (5th Generation), as well as two other completely new printers, the Replicator Mini and the Replicator Z18 (see figure 5.1). There is a great deal of similarity under the hoods of these systems, with the primary difference being the size of the print area. The Replicator Mini has a total print area of 10 cm by 10 cm by 12.5 cm, or roughly 3.9 inches by 3.9 inches by 4.9 inches, almost identical to the print volume of the original Cupcake CNC printer. The Replicator (5th Generation) has a print area of 25.2 cm by 19.9 cm by 15 cm, more than six times the volume of the Mini. But the true behemoth in the MakerBot lineup is the Z18 (see figure 5.2), with a massive build area of 30.5 cm by 30.5 cm by 45.7 cm, or 12 inches by 12 inches by 18 inches. That final height measurement is where the Z18 gets its name, for the maximum print height on the Z axis.

Other than those print volume differences, the specifications for the swath of 5th Generation printers from MakerBot are surprisingly similar. They share the same newly-redesigned extruder, they are all designed for PLA filament, they all have a camera, and each uses the MakerBot Desktop software to print.

The choice between the three printers really depends on the question "How large a part do you want to print?" (or possibly how many smaller objects you want to print simultaneously). Either way, it's about the size of the build plate, and each step up the levels of printer with MakerBot carries a fairly substantial price increase. The Mini retails for $1,375, the Replicator (5th Generation) for $2,899, and the Z18

Figure 5.2
The Replicator Z18

for an unbelievable $6,499. Those prices don't include MakerBot's enhanced support service or warranty that they call MakerCare, which brings the prices up by $150, $350, and $750, respectively.

For the time being, MakerBot is still selling the Replicator 2 and the Replicator 2X, for $2,199 and $2,799 respectively. It is unclear how long these older models will remain for sale, but both are still very capable printers. The technology differences between these and the 5th Generation models have less to do with the quality of the prints possible and more to do with the management possibilities and the future of the 5th Generation platform.

For the majority of libraries looking at which 3-D printer to buy, MakerBot is the right answer. MakerBot's printers have the largest install base, they provide an option for enhanced support (which libraries without someone fairly technical on staff will need), and the printers themselves are solid and reliable. They are not, however, open and interchangeable with other types of 3-D printers. If you are dedicated to using open-source software or prefer interchangeability in your hardware, MakerBot printers may be less of a good thing.

MakerBot
http://makerbot.com

Figure 5.3
The LulzBot TAZ

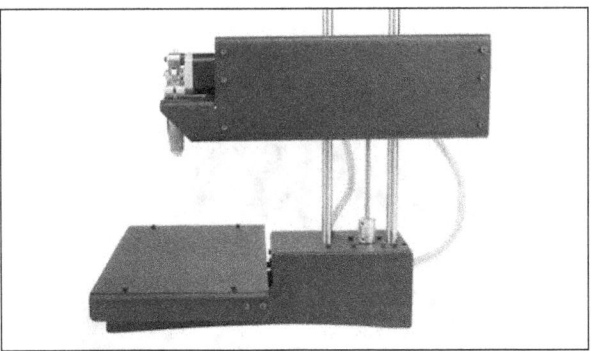

Figure 5.4
The Printrbot Simple

Figure 5.5
The Printrbot Plus

Pretty much every other printer on this list uses open-source software as its print engine, and the majority of them are open hardware as well. Sticking with open source for your 3-D printer ensures that you will be able to update your printer later without huge changes to your workflow and that if you need replacement parts you can often purchase them from a variety of sources. While MakerBot is probably the right answer for the majority of libraries right now, that will not be the case for every library, and it will not be the case forever.

LulzBot

LulzBot is a 3-D printer company based in Loveland, Colorado, that is dedicated to producing printers that are completely open. Its flagship printer, the TAZ 3 (see figure 5.3), is an open-hardware and open-software printer, with everything from the firmware to the corner brackets open and shareable. This is, obviously, very different in business model from the MakerBot family of printers.

The TAZ 3 has the best price-to-print build plate area of any printer anywhere. The TAZ has a build plate area of 298 mm by 275 mm by 250 mm, or 11.7 inches by 10.8 inches by 9.8 inches, slightly smaller than the MakerBot Z18, but the TAZ retails for $2,149, less than a third of the cost of the Z18. It will also print in a much wider variety of filaments, since it has a heated build plate. As a matter of fact, LulzBot specifically advertises the TAZ as capable of printing nearly any filament you throw at it. In the description for the TAZ, LulzBot specifically calls attention to the fact that it can print in PLA, ABS, PVA, polystyrene, nylon, and more.

The downside of the design of the TAZ is that it's totally an exposed build-plate design, which makes temperature control very difficult in the area around the build plate. This isn't limited to the TAZ; most 3-D printers don't ship with an enclosed print area by default, but it is a downside that can affect the reliability of printing, especially with ABS or other temperature-sensitive plastics.

I would say that the LulzBot TAZ 3 would be a great 3-D printer for a library that has been working with an older Replicator or other printer and has the in-house knowledge to take advantage of the open nature of it. But if you don't think your staff will be doing significant upgrades or maintenance to the printer, it may not be the right printer for you.

LulzBot
www.lulzbot.com

Figure 5.6
Solidoodle's 4th Generation 3-D printer

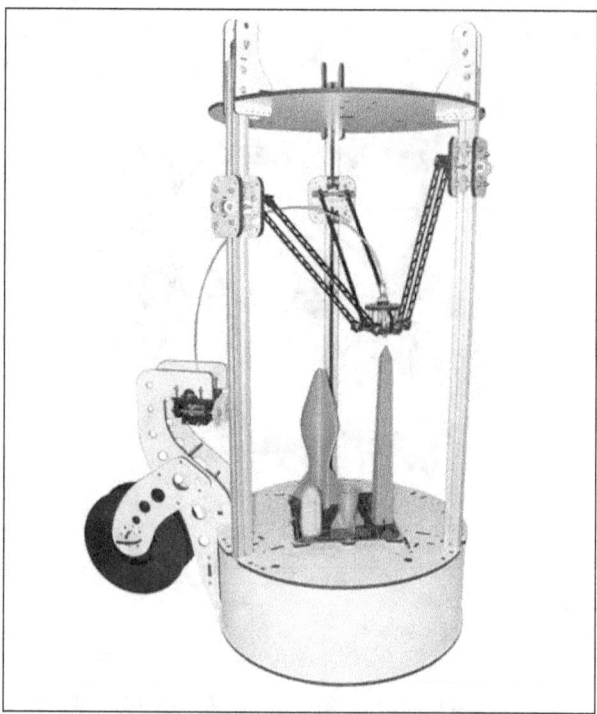

Figure 5.7
SeeMeCNC's Rostock Max

Printrbot

Printrbot makes two different models of 3-D printers, the Printrbot Simple and the Printrbot Plus (see figures 5.4 and 5.5). The main difference in the two is, again, size of build plate. The Printrbot Simple is designed as an entry-level 3-D printer, with a print area of 150 mm by 150 mm by 150 mm, or 6 inches by 6 inches by 6 inches. The Simple prints only in PLA but is available, assembled and ready to print, for only $599. The Printrbot Plus is a larger printer, with a 10-inch-by-10-inch-by-10-inch print area, also only for PLA. The Printrbot Plus retails for $1,299, a fantastic deal for the print volume, although limited in print material options.

Printrbot
http://printrbot.com

Solidoodle

Solidoodle, which has been around for a few years now, was one of the first companies to build and ship a fully assembled, non-kit 3-D printer. Its current model, the Solidoodle 4th Generation (see figure 5.6), is a PLA- and ABS-capable printer, with an 8-inch-by-8-inch-by-8-inch build platform. It comes ready to print for $999, and Solidoodle's older model (the 3rd Generation), with the same build plate size but a slightly less aesthetically pleasing case design, sells for only $799.

Solidoodle
www.solidoodle.com

SeeMeCNC Rostock Max and Orion

The printers sold by SeeMeCNC are a very different breed of fused deposition printer. They are the only delta-style printers on the list, as opposed to the Cartesian style of the rest of the pack. The Rostock Max (see figure 5.7) has an 11-inch-diameter print bed (delta printer beds are measured in diameter, as they are circular rather than rectangular), with a vertical height of 14.5 inches, one of the largest overall volumes available on an FDM printer. But I wouldn't recommend the kit to anyone who didn't have some experience with complicated electronic builds. The positive thing about buying the kit is the price, which at $999, gives you a huge amount of value for the money, but you will have to put a few dozen hours into building it.

The Orion, however, is a fully assembled delta-style printer (see figure 5.8). Smaller than the Max, with only a 6-inch diameter and 9-inch height print area, it comes pre-assembled and ready to print. The

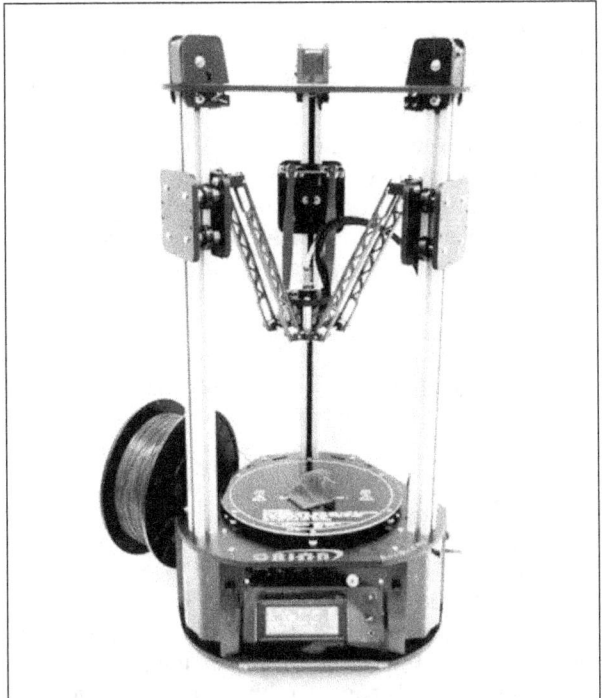

Figure 5.8
SeeMeCNC's Orion

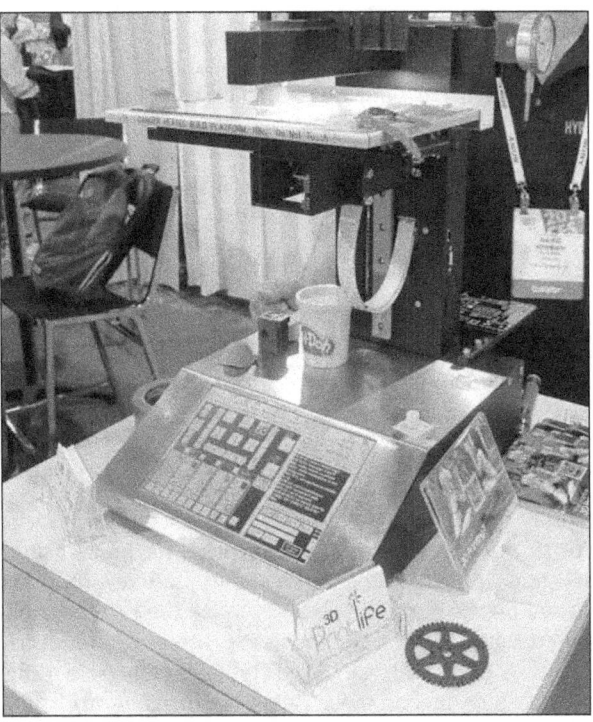

Figure 5.9
The Hyrel System 30 printing in Play-Doh

quality of a delta 3-D printer is nearly identical to that of a Cartesian style, but they are amazingly cool to watch. Check out the YouTube video of a Rostock Max printing if you want an idea of how they look in action.

Both of these are well-designed and solid choices for printing in a library, but the fact that delta printers are far more unusual and that one of them is kit-only means that I don't expect these to take the world by storm. They are extraordinarily cool, though.

SeeMeCNC
http://seemecnc.com

YouTube: Rostock Max printing
https://www.youtube.com/watch?v=k--r3C8Hu7A

Hyrel 3D

One of my favorite 3-D printers that I've had a chance to see over the last year is the Hyrel System 30. Hyrel 3D manufactures a variety of printers, but the System 30 is the one that really is worth exploring. At first glance, it appears to be just a high-end FDM printer, with the typical enhancements for a high-end FDM, such as an enclosed build area, a heated build plate, a 225-mm-by-200-mm-by-200-mm build area, and a printhead that is capable of printing PLA, ABS, nylon, and other plastics. In addition, the System 30 includes a full Linux computer embedded in the printer, complete with a touchscreen LCD. This means that you can not only control the printer, but the printer itself will do the slicing and plating, obviating the need for a secondary computer at all. You can load an STL file directly into the system, and it will take it from there.

But the real secret sauce for the System 30 is in the swappable printheads. The printer really is a printing system, as it supports up to four FDM printheads being mounted simultaneously. Yes, it can simultaneously print in four different filaments. The thing that really makes the System 30 stand out, though, is the EMO-25 optional extruder. The EMO-25 is a sort of industrial syringe that is computer-controlled and can be loaded with any putty-like material as a printing substrate. With the System 30 and the EMO-25, you can make 3-D prints literally in Silly Putty. Or in clay. Or, my personal favorite, in Sugru, an air-curable rubber. When I was able to play with a System 30 at CES 2014, they were making little 3-D printed houses out of Play-Doh (see figure 5.9). And that printing ability is just interchangeable with a traditional FDM printhead, so you don't lose capabilities.

All of this is available at a base price of $3,995, with additional FDM extruders costing $250 and the EMO-25 syringe-style printhead at $225 for a basic and $300 for a professional kit. The professional kit includes an extra barrel for the syringe cylinder so that you can reload the material for printing while a print is happening, then swap when it runs out, thus allowing for larger prints of unusual materials. So it is far more expensive than most of the rest of the printers I've highlighted, but it is also a more robust and flexible machine. I'd love to see what sorts of things a good children's librarian could do with the ability to arbitrarily create 3-D objects from Play-Doh.

Hyrel 3D
www.hyrel3d.com

Cubify

Cubify makes a series of printers, but it is best known for its attempt to simplify the process for home users. Its goal appears to be to create Apple-like products, heavy on the design aspects, to make the printer itself an attractive gadget for the home. It features an auto-leveling print bed, cartridge-style filament reloading (which also means it isn't capable of using arbitrary filament purchased elsewhere), and Wi-Fi connectivity for remote printing. The Cube (see figure 5.10) has a 140-mm-by-140-mm-by-140-mm print area and is capable of printing in both PLA and ABS.

The Cube retails for $1,299, and while it may be the most attractive of the 3-D printers that I've listed, it's also the least flexible. My main concern for libraries would be the cartridge-style filament loading, as it locks you into being able to purchase only directly from Cubify, so that you won't be able to take advantage of the variety of filaments available on the open market. And, of course, if Cubify goes out of business, it may leave you with the inability to purchase new filament altogether.

Cubify is trying to create an ecosystem for its printers, in the same sort of way that MakerBot has. It has a cloud service that stores STL files for printing, as well as a store from which you can purchase printable files for output to your Cube. Cubify clearly wants a closed ecosystem, again in the Apple vein, where it owns the entire stack of the ecosystem of 3-D printing. It hasn't been successful at that just yet, but its solution might be reasonable for some libraries.

Cubify
http://cubify.com

Formlabs

The Formlabs Form 1 (see figure 5.11) is the first consumer-level stereolithography printer. This makes it both amazing, because it can print at nearly ludicrous resolutions (see figure 5.12), and terrible, because the consumable resin is considerably more expensive than the plastic filament that FDM printers use. The build area is smaller than that of most FDM printers, at only 125 mm by 125 mm by 165 mm, but the minimum layer thickness is only 25 microns, a quarter the height of the best FDM printers.

Formlabs sells three colors of resin that work with the Form 1, clear, grey, and white. The resin sells for $149 per liter, which is roughly three times the cost for the same amount of PLA filament for an FDM printer. Because Formlabs is the first out of the starting gate with SLA printing for the consumer, other companies are beginning to sell resin that they list as "compatible with the Form 1." This resin is almost always much cheaper than that offered directly from Formlabs; a

Figure 5.10
The Cubify Cube

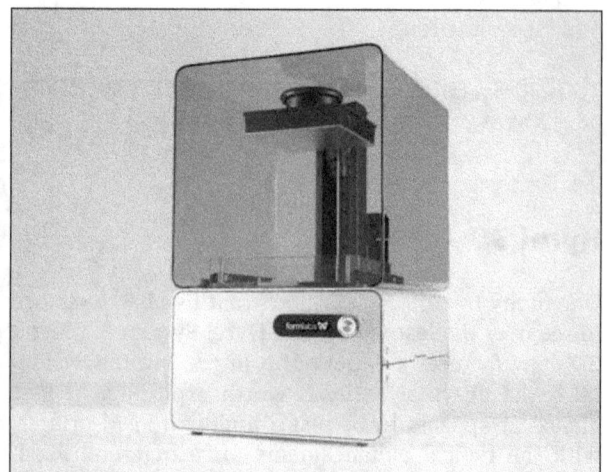

Figure 5.11
The Formlabs Form 1

Figure 5.12
A tiny, intricate figure printed with the Form 1

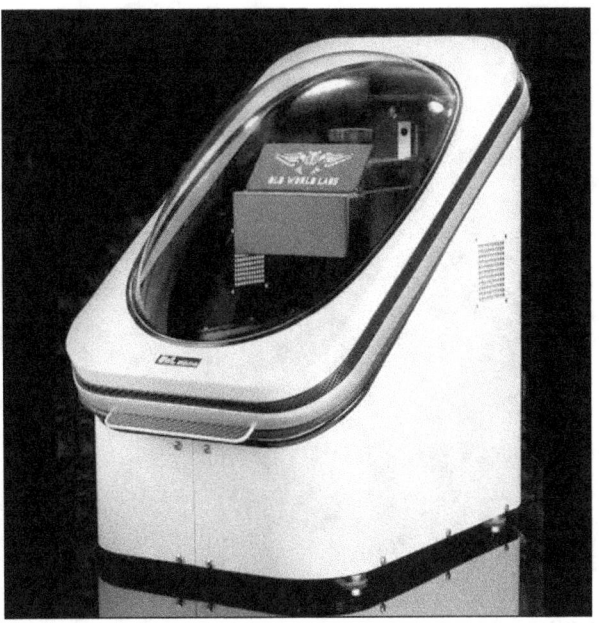

Figure 5.13
The OWL Nano

quick look around shows that said resin is about two-thirds the price of the Formlabs resin, and it's available in many more colors.

I think that SLA printers may become far more common in libraries over the next few years, especially as competition heats up and more companies begin selling their own versions of this technology. Because they can print geometries that are difficult for FDM printers, and the parts they produce are far more finished in look and feel (see figure 5.12), it's a natural progression. The Form 1 retails for $3,299, well within the budgets of many libraries that might want to play with the next generation of 3-D printers.

Formlabs
http://formlabs.com

Old World Laboratories

A very recent entry into the stereolithography game, Old World Laboratories, showed off its printer, the OWL Nano (see figure 5.13), at CES 2014. The OWL Nano has a slightly larger build area than the Form 1, at 150 mm by 150 mm by 200 mm, and it uses a slightly different technique for aiming the laser that gives it a claimed .1 micron layer detail height. The OWL Nano is more expensive than the Form 1, at $4,900, and I'm guessing that most of that is due to the scale of the company, given that many of the underlying systems are likely the same.

In addition to the incredible layer detail, the OWL Nano uses a generic photopolymer, which should mean that the consumables for printing are less expensive over time. Given a drop in price for the photopolymer, the printer itself actually has fewer moving parts than an FDM printer and might be a better long-term-use machine than something like the MakerBot models. It just isn't quite there in terms of price yet.

Old World Laboratories
http://oldworldlabs.com

Mcor

The last specific 3-D printer that I want to talk about is the Mcor Technologies IRIS, the only example of laminated object manufacturing that I've had a chance to examine. The IRIS is a LOM printer that uses plain copy paper as its printing substrate, with a full-color ink-jet printer as a part of the process that enables full color 3-D printing at very inexpensive costs per print. It produces prints that have a layer height the same as the thickness of a sheet of paper because the layers are literally sheets of paper.

The results of the printer are remarkably sturdy and solid. Unlike FDM-printed models, the objects that come off of the IRIS are solid and quite hefty. The glue used is just a basic wood glue, like the Elmer's Glue you remember from your childhood, except a little thinner. As a result, the layers are very solidly

Figure 5.14
An object printed on the Mcor Technologies IRIS

put together, and the objects really do feel like a solid piece of wood (see figure 5.14).

If LOM prints are solid, high quality, and full color, then what's the downside? The downside is the fact that it's still a commercial and not consumer technology, which means that the price is still very high for the printer itself. Mcor Technologies doesn't list a price on the website (always a sign that it is more than you want to pay), but in discussion at CES 2014, I was told that its printers started around $35,000. Yes, you read that right. So it's clearly not something that every library could even think of affording, especially as an experiment. But again, as the price drops and the technology becomes more common, this might be an interesting type of printer to keep an eye on.

Mcor Technologies IRIS
www.mcortechnologies.com/3-D-printers/iris

Notes

Keep up with
Library Technology
REPORTS

Upcoming Issues	
August/ September 50:6	**Digital Media Labs in Libraries** by Amanda Goodman
October 50:7	**Social Media Curation** by Joyce Kasman Valenza, Brenda L. Boyer, Della Curtis
November/ December 50:8	**Selecting and Evaluating the Best Mobile Apps for Library Services** by Nicole Hennig

Subscribe
alatechsource.org/subscribe

Purchase single copies in the ALA Store
alastore.ala.org

alatechsource.org

ALA TechSource, a unit of the publishing department of the American Library Association

www.ingramcontent.com/pod-product-compliance
Lightning Source LLC
Chambersburg PA
CBHW080846020526
44115CB00034B/2950